FASCINA...
FACES

Most animals have faces.
Some faces are funny.
Some faces are creepy.
Some faces are friendly,
and some faces are tricky.

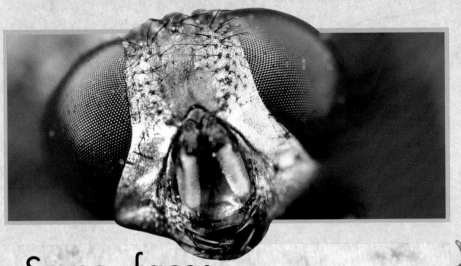

Some faces
have lumps and bumps,
and lots of eyes
in funny places.

4

Some faces
have bulging eyes
and a hungry mouth,
and gills for
breathing in and out.

7

Some animals come
out at night!
Their faces have eyes
that shine in the light.

Some faces have funny noses.
Some faces have whiskers.
And some faces look as if
they are wearing face paint!

Some faces are hard to spot.
They try to look
like things around them.

13

Baby faces come
in lots of ways.
Some are wrinkly.
Some are fuzzy.
Baby faces are
cute and cuddly.

15

Faces are fascinating.
Faces are fun.
Can you make one?